WISDOM CANDY
Consolation for Families That Suffer a Loss

Book One

by Doctor Barry A. Goodfield

Edited by Mike Riley

Published by
The Goodfield Institute

Written and Illustrated by Goodfield, Barry A.
Edited by Mike Riley

WISDOM CANDY
Consolation for Families That Suffer a Loss
First Edition; Book One of the Wisdom Candy series

ISBN # 978-0-9969899-7-8
Library of Congress Control Number: 2016946918

Published by The Goodfield Institute LLC

Table of Contents:

Foreword

Dr. Barry Goodfield first created this book as a series of gifts to his daughter. Each self-illustrated story by this internationally renowned psychotherapist was meant to provide her with understanding and consolation in the face of a loss.

The first story in book one helped his daughter Jane Felice to understand why her birth meant so much to her parents. It also explains how her parents dealt with the miscarriage and loss of the infant whose conception had preceded Jane Felice's own delivery.

The second story in Wisdom Candy book two helped Jane Felice to accept the death of her grandmother. It also explains some of the values which Barry wished to pass on to his daughter. One of Saint Paul's epistles names three Divine Gifts: "And now faith, hope, and love abide, these three; and the greatest of these is love." Doctor Goodfield strongly retains his own faith, as well as a powerful hopefulness and charity for all of mankind.

Doctor Goodfield intended the final story to serve his whole family whenever the stresses or traumas of the day made it difficult to find refuge and recovery in sleep, and in its healing handmaiden of dreams.

Barry recently asked me what I thought of these works. I was inspired by the universal appeal of the teachings they adroitly convey. His work makes important life lessons seem like childs' play. From the death of the unborn to the loss of the long-loved, these stories and their lessons make palatable, digestible morsels out of the wisdom that comes with maturity and deep insight.

His stories make the best possible bedtime stories for children who are coping with grief.

Michael D. "Mike" Riley, MSJ
Glendale, Arizona USA

Preface

I've been a psychotherapist for more than 40 years. But I think in cartoons much of the time.

So like any family man facing all the issues of life's process, I needed to explain them to myself and to my family as these issues occurred, with all of the pain and questions that accompany them.

These two little stories were my way of explaining to my young daughter, Jane Felice, big issues in a way that she might understand — and I have to admit, that I might as well.

Dr. Barry A. Goodfield, PhD
Glendale, Arizona USA

Author's Dedication

To my wife Dori. She truly is my angel who makes angels: you are simply the best person I know.

To our daughter's Godparents, Jane and Francois. It was Jane who gave me the idea of an angel that was not yet ready for life here on earth.

To Mort Rosenblum, my life-long pal, who held his ground and his phone while listening to me rant and rave at our loss. He was there when I reached out in despair.

To our Rev. Dan White from our little Presbyterian Church on the hill in San Rafael, California. It was he who gave God a human voice that provided us with perspective and relief.

And finally, to our little BoBo, our precious daughter Jane Felice. Mommy and I will try to live by and raise you with the ten life lessons I've told here. These stories are yours as much as ours.

Chapter One

The Scene:

Paradise Construction Company

The Scene:

Paradise Construction Company

Oh, look! Maybe those two people might want me — even though I'm not really ready yet.

The Scene:

Descending

Please, Oh Lord,
Send us a Little Angel
to have and to love.

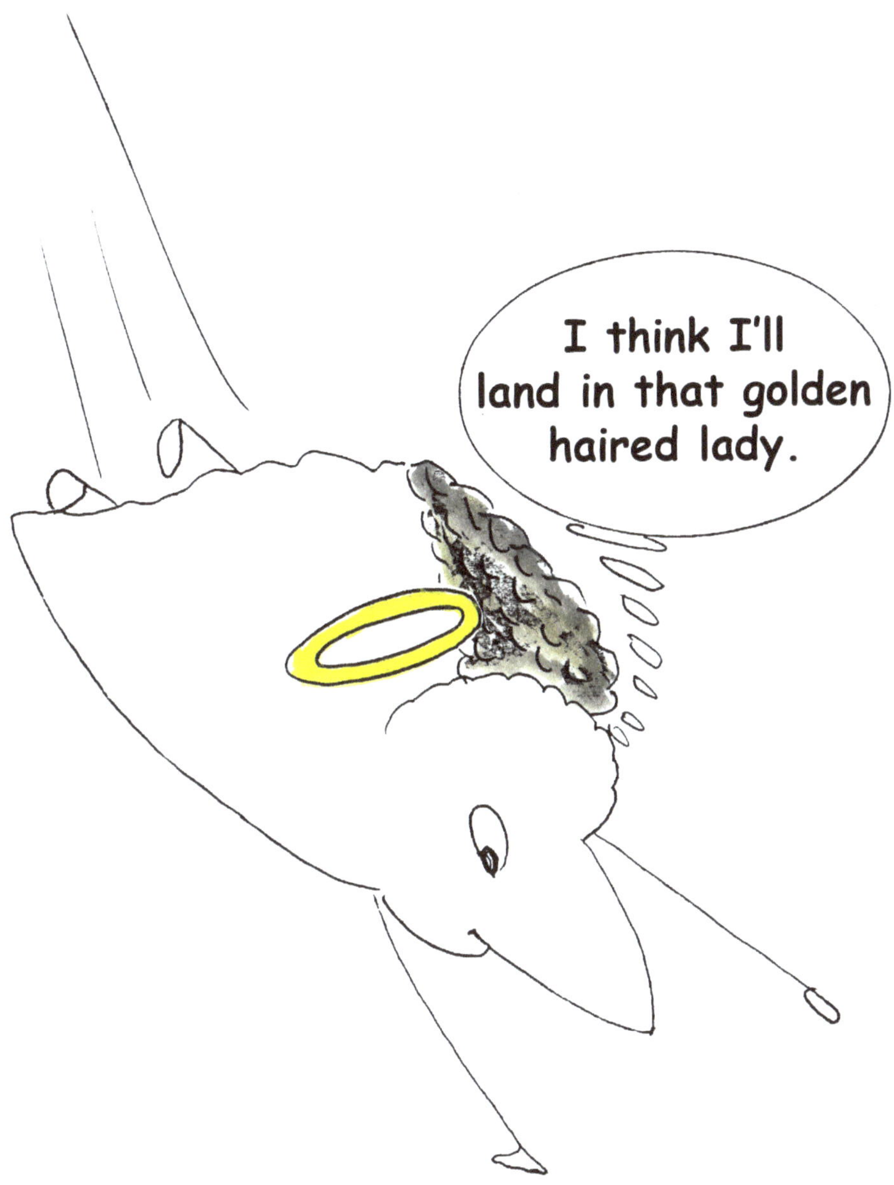
I think I'll
land in that golden
haired lady.

I've got great news for you, darling! We're going to have a baby!
WOW! Marvelous! Amazing! Miraculous!

I am as happy as I can be!
I am as happy as a pig in poop!

The Scene:

Paradise Construction Company

The Scene:

OP CENTER FARU
("Fallen Angels Recovery Unit")

Aha! There she is! She sleeps in the tummy of the lady with long golden hair.

Sometimes I hate this job. But God knows best.

Yeah. I'm putting in for a transfer out of FARU!

C'mon, little one.
We have to go home.
It's not your time yet.

Dear God, please.
Let me return to earth when you think I'm ready.
Please...please...they're nice people and I'll be
the best little girl you ever created!
Please, oh Lord, please...

Okay, little angel.
You can return.

The Scene:
In Heaven

I'm so very, very sad!
I'm so very, very angry!
#!#!#*

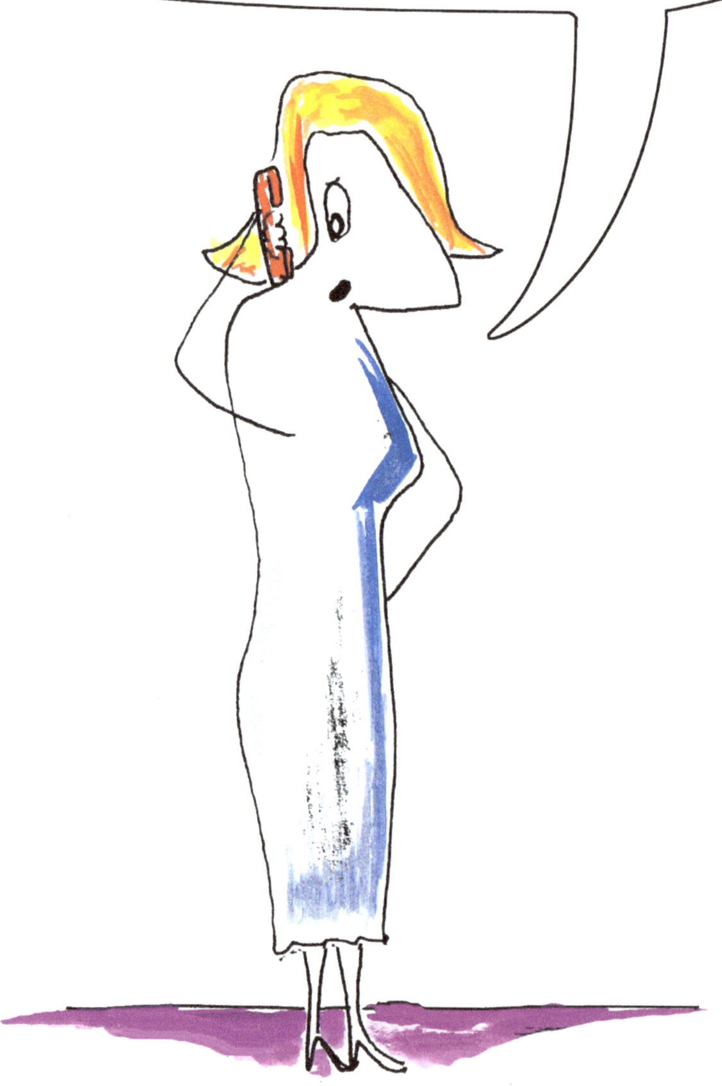
Hi, friends. Yes, it's Jane...yes, I heard.
Can I suggest some thoughts for your comfort?
Think of it this way: children are gifts.
Gifts from God.
Your little lost angel just wasn't ready yet.
She's been called back to heaven 'til
she's ready to return to you.

That makes sense.
Maybe it will be the
same one as before, with
a new wing. Or maybe God
will send an entirely new one
Only He knows.

With time,
life's tears and rage
turn silent, replaced with
muted memories of
stormier days.

Eventually, the sun
bursts through the
clouds, and then...

Chapter Two

IT'S BOBO AND THE BEANSTALK

I'm off to be with
the golden-haired lady
and her man with
the hat.
EXIT

How do I get down from Heaven? On that beanstalk thingy?
That "beanstalk", as you call it, is made of wishes, will, love and prayers. It connects Heaven and Earth.

Will I have what I need to survive and to grow?
Of course. You'll have the past, this time, as well as the future, all wrapped up in this moment, or "now". It's what God calls "the Present."

Don't worry, kid. You'll get all that stuff when you check out before you leave.
Just pick it up over there at the Values Store.
You know, it's no wonder that so many don't make it in life. They forget all of the gifts and necessities they're given at the Values Store..

Paradise Construction Company
Values Store Entrance
ALWAYS push your limits. Be a great risk-taker!
Feel your boundaries. NEVER let anyone overwhelm them!

Paradise Construction Company
Refusals Department
Refuse to accept the unacceptable. When you accept the unacceptable, you tell others it's really okay to do whatever they want to do to you.

Paradise Construction Company
Yes and No Department
You can never trust somebody's "yes" if you can't trust their "no".

Paradise Construction Company
Trust and Perception Department
Trust your feelings. They are NEVER wrong!
Your perception of people or events may not be correct. They're simply one person's translation of the world.

Paradise Construction Company
Contact and Method Department
Stay able to make real contact and always do it in a way that feels right for you.

Paradise Construction Company
Honesty Department
Never lie to yourself about your needs, desires, or motives.
Life will be hard sometimes, but it will be better and clearer in general.

Paradise Construction Company
Courage Department
Don't just stand your ground. Move forward!
My favorite four-letter word is "DOIT"!

Paradise Construction Company
Check Out Stand

Relax, little one. You may forget some of these things, but that's what parents and friends are for.

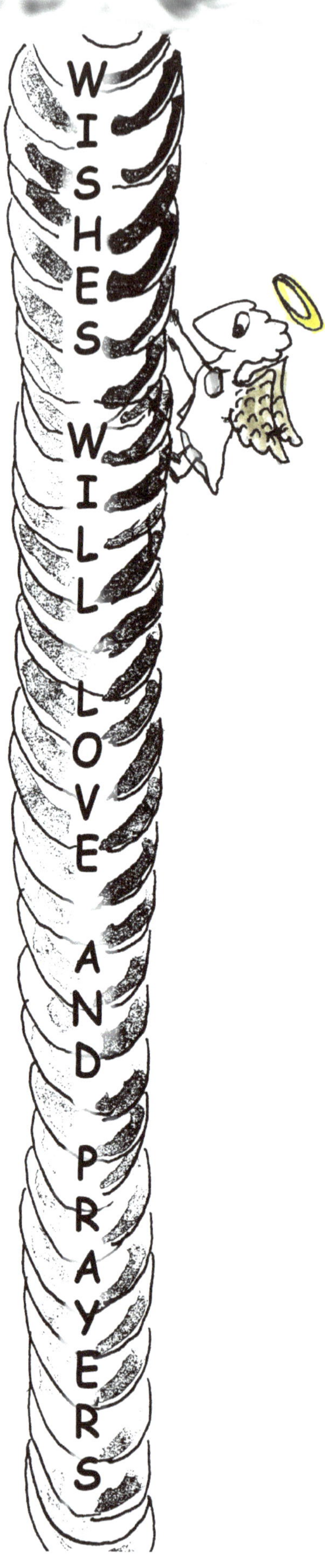
WISHES WILL LOVE AND PRAYERS

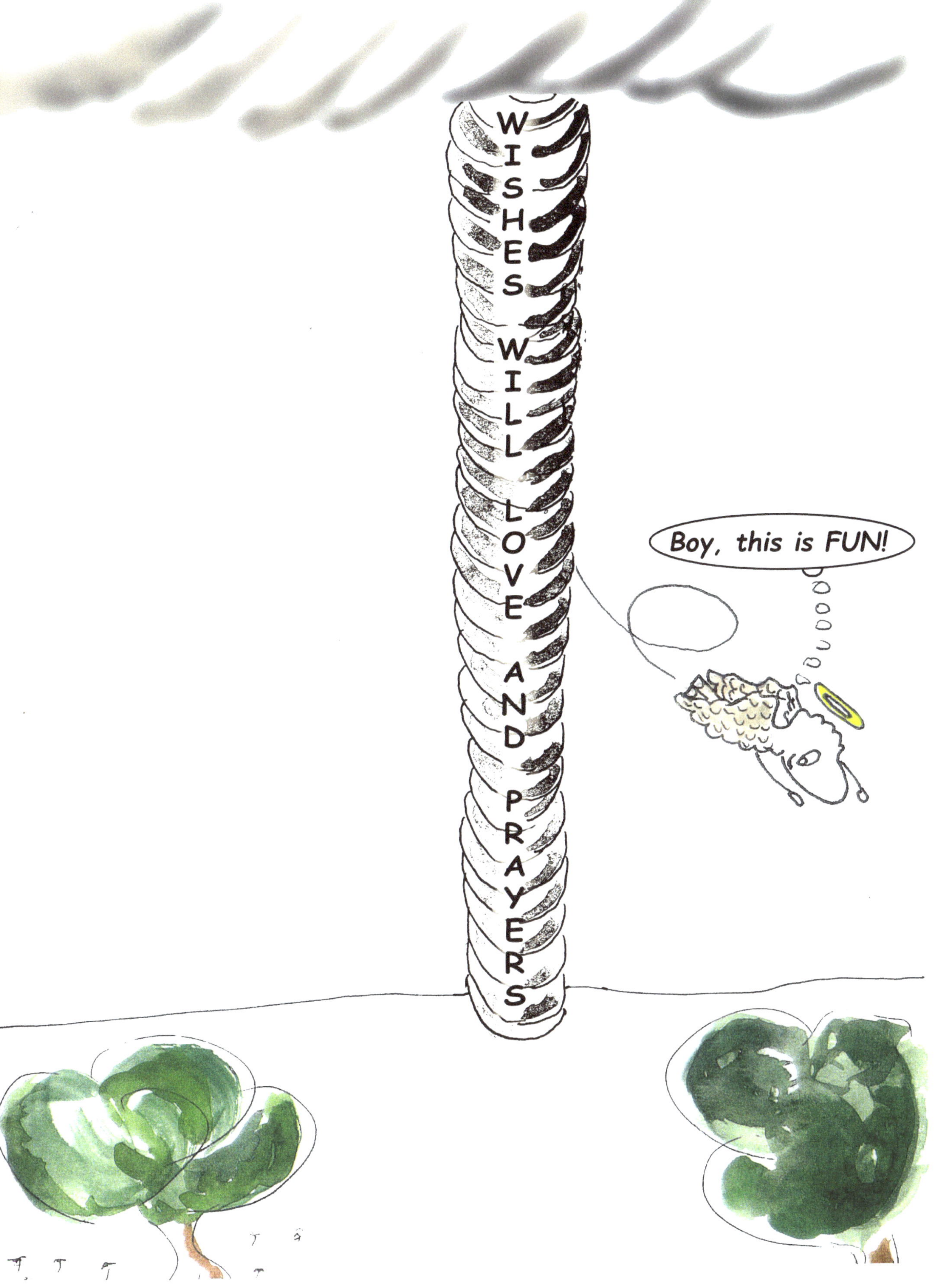
WISHES WILL LOVE AND PRAYERS
Boy, this is FUN!

Okay, there she is!
The lady with the long golden hair!
I'm coming home!

I have an angel inside. This time I know nothing will go wrong. I can feel it!
We'll plan everything down to the last detail!

It's exactly 13 minutes to the hospital. Everything's all set!
This is great! I've got the best food and no smoke or alcohol. What a good Mommy!

THE BIG DAY...

Okay, I locked the house. Let's go!
Got the car keys for me?
They're in the house.
What do we do now?
38

Don't worry! I'll climb the fence! Oh, no! HELP! I'm hung up!

Ten frantic, frenzied, furious, frenetic minutes later...

Here's your little angel!

Fallen Angel Recovery Unit
(OP Center FARU)
There she is, sleeping in the arms of the lady with the long golden hair. The daddy with the big hat is looking on, smiling.
I love this job. God really does know best.
Yeah. I'm going to hold off on asking for that transfer out of here.

You know, not everybody gets the joy of a baby after they have a miscarriage.
So how does that work?

Lord knows I'm not God. But I have been hanging around these Pearly Gates for eons. Here's my humble "not God" opinion.
Tell him how you see it: those who do not have a child later have an even more important mission in life.

They must turn pain into understanding and knowledge into wisdom. For most people this is the most difficult test of all.

They must create within themselves an even deeper appreciation of how special life is for us all.

You know that tears don't wash away pain. They help us to see new and better ways of fixing pain and loss.

People who suffer a loss can become the best teachers of love and understanding.

The message is clear. Life on Earth is one big school. We learn and teach life's big lessons. We are both students and teachers alike.
We still have lots to learn, that's for sure!

A Baaad Bedtime Story

The One Sheep Lesson

I can't sleep!

Look, young lady. You're having an Econo-Dream. Or shall I say pre-dream. It comes with only one sheep. That's me.

How am I going to go to sleep with an Econo-dream and one dumb sheep?

Okay, you are kinda cute. If you were real, I could snuggle up and then I could sleep. But the problem is you aren't real.

Listen, sheep! I'm not looking for some philosophical debate. I just want to get some sleep! Is that too much for you to get through that fuzzy head of yours?

So, what do I have to lose?
I believe the impossible CAN
become possible.
I really do!

Wow! Believing in the impossible dream sure is tiring! Let's get some rest.

www.ingramcontent.com/pod-product-compliance
Lightning Source LLC
LaVergne TN
LVHW070141110826
845147LV00002B/305
* 9 7 8 0 9 9 6 9 8 9 9 7 8 *